POCKET PRAYERS
for WOMEN

Simple Prayers
of
Faith

 Publications International, Ltd.

Authors: Natalie Walker Whitlock, Alisa Hope Wagner

Additional contributors: Nancy Parker Brummett, Pam Campbell, Elaine Wright Colvin, Elaine Creasman, Christine A. Dallman, June Eaton, Lain Chroust Ehmann, Margaret Anne Huffman, Marie D. Jones, Randy Petersen, Carol McAdoo Rehme, Carol Stigger, Gary Wilde

Cover Art: Shutterstock.com

Interior Art: Getty, Shutterstock.com

ISBN: 978-1-4508-8299-6

Manufactured in China.

8 7 6 5 4 3 2 1

Pray Anywhere, Anytime

Humans have a deep desire to converse with their Creator. Whether we're praising or questioning, we want to reach out to our God.

Pocket Prayers for Women: Simple Prayers of Faith is a tool for daily conversation with God. It includes prayers—both classic and modern—about faith. You will also find brief passages of Scripture and inspirational quotes to keep you strong in faith during good and trying times.

Best of all, this book is small enough to fit in a purse, briefcase, glove box, or nightstand—making it easy for you to take advantage of the awesome privilege of talking with God every day!

3

Time for God

Who is like you, Lord God Almighty?
You, Lord, are mighty, and your
faithfulness surrounds you.

Psalm 89:8 NIV

I want to draw closer to you, Lord, to immerse myself in your faithfulness. Getting to know you will take effort and sacrifice on my part, though, and in today's culture, time seems limited. People feel they have precious little time with family and friends; time with God seems nearly impossible. Help me to adjust my busy schedule and find creative ways to spend time with you.

I can spend time with you during my drive to work or the grocery store. I can spend time with you while I exercise or fold laundry. I can spend time with you while I take a shower or cook dinner.

I don't want to miss quality time with you, Lord, due to time constraints or my preconceived notions of how prayer should be. Many times life is hectic and full of distractions, but I will keep my eyes focused on you and my ears ready to listen.

Mere "Stuff"

*Do not store up for yourselves treasures
on earth, where moth and rust consume
and where thieves break in and steal;
but store up for yourselves treasures
in heaven, where neither moth nor rust
consumes and where thieves do not break
in and steal. For where your treasure is,
there your heart will be also.*

Matthew 6:19–21

*L*ord, I know "it's only stuff," but
much of it is useful, and I want
to take good care of it. Help me see
the line between wanting to be a good
steward and caring too much about
material things. Help me be a responsible
caretaker without putting too much
value on mere "stuff."

The Best Laid Plans

Trust in the Lord with all your heart,
and do not rely on your own insight.

Proverbs 3:5

*L*ord, how it must amuse you
when we attempt to orchestrate
the details of our days as if everything
were under our control. It's only when
you are involved in our plans that things
go smoothly. Teach us to trust your way,
even when we can't see how every detail
will turn out. Our insight is only as good
as our reliance on you. Please be with us
each day, Lord.

If you want to make God laugh,
tell him your plans.

—Anonymous

The Faith of the Ages

No distrust made him waver
concerning the promise of God,
but he grew strong in his faith as he gave
glory to God, being fully convinced that
God was able to do what he had promised.

Romans 4:20–21

Father God, when I'm tempted to give up on a task, it helps to read about Abraham, Moses, Joseph, David, Job—all those whose times of trial and perseverance are so beautifully preserved for us through your Word. Once we are attuned to your plan for our lives, we can continue on with the certainty that you always complete what you start. We can stand firmly on your promises, confident

that you will give us the strength we
need to keep going.

Thank you for the faith of the ages, Lord!
It is also the faith for today.

> *Faith goes up the stairs that love has*
> *made and looks out of the windows*
> *which hope has opened.*
> —Charles Haddon Spurgeon

A Committed Heart and Soul

[Jesus] called the crowd with his disciples, and said to them, "If any want to become my followers, let them deny themselves and take up their cross and follow me.... For what will it profit them to gain the whole world and forfeit their life?"

Mark 8:34, 36

Jesus, your purposes are generally the opposite of an earthbound here-and-now mind-set. This verse makes it clear that it takes a committed heart and soul to follow you. Where I have become rusty in my attentiveness in following you, please refresh me with the breath of your Spirit.

Free Beings

And without faith it is impossible to please God, for whoever would approach him must believe that he exists and that he rewards those who seek him.

Hebrews 11:6

There is plenty of evidence for the existence of God, but if we could actually prove it, we wouldn't need faith. God left room for us to be free beings, and freedom is what brings creativity, invention, and interest to the world.

Understanding is the reward of faith. So do not seek to understand in order to believe, but believe so that you may understand.

—Augustine of Hippo

Songs of Praise

I will praise you with the harp for your faithfulness, my God; I will sing praise to you with the lyre, Holy One of Israel.

Psalm 71:22 NIV

I might not be able to praise you with an instrument, Lord, but I can still thank you for your faithfulness.

When I'm folding laundry, I can praise you for the clothes on my back. When I'm stuck in traffic, I can praise you for the beautiful scenery around me. When I'm fighting illness, I can praise you for the Spirit you breathed into me. And when the people I love struggle, I can praise you for bringing such wonderful people into my life.

This gift of life is precious, and I know my eternity is secure in you. Though my days are not always easy, I know that you stay faithfully by my side—guiding my steps and filling my heart with joy.

I praise you with all the resources at my disposal, Lord. I know that you treasure the motive of my praise—not the means.

Who He Is

God said, "This is the sign of the covenant
that I make between me and you and every
living creature that is with you,
for all future generations: I have set my
bow in the clouds, and it shall be a sign of
the covenant between me and the earth."

Genesis 9:12–13

God gave the rainbow as a sign
of his promise to never flood
the entire earth again. The colors that
spread out in spectrum, as sunlight
passes through water droplets in the sky,
speak of God's faithfulness in keeping
his promise to Noah and to all the
generations that have followed.

Faithfulness marks God's character. It is who he is, through and through. Let every rainbow we see remind us of God's faithful love, and let praise flow from our hearts to the one who always keeps his promises.

Lord, thank you for rainbows and all other reminders of your faithful love to me. Open my eyes to see each one today so I can delight in your promises and give you praise.

Entrust the Big Things to God

*And what does the Lord require of you
but to do justice, and to love kindness,
and to walk humbly with your God?*

Micah 6:8

*L*ord, we pray for all those in positions of leadership in our government. The pressures and influences on them are of a magnitude we can only imagine. Watch over them, Lord. Reach out to them with your grace, and instill in them your priorities and your vision for our country and our world.

*It's hard to stay angry at someone
for whom you pray.*

Safe Now and for Eternity

The Lord is good, a stronghold on a day of trouble; he protects those who take refuge in him, even in a rushing flood.

Nahum 1:7–8

Thank you, Lord, for the fact that when difficulties start to accumulate like waters at flood stage, I can find the high ground of safety in you. Today I trust your goodness as well as your promises of protection. Even if everything I own is swept away in the flood, I know you will still be here with me. Remind me that the stuff of this world is temporary, but my life in you is safe both now and for eternity.

Light of Love

The Lord exists for ever;
your word is firmly fixed in heaven.
Your word is a lamp to my feet
and a light to my path.

Psalm 119:89, 105

God! Thou art love! I build my faith
on that....
I know thee, who hast kept my path,
and made
Light for me in darkness, tempering
sorrow
So that it reached me like a solemn joy;
It were too strange that I should doubt
thy love.

—Robert Browning, "Paracelsus"

O Word of God Incarnate, O Wisdom from
* on high,*
O Truth unchanged, unchanging, O Light
* of our dark sky:*

We praise thee for the radiance
That from the hallowed page,
A lantern to our footsteps,
Shines on from age to age.

  —William W. How, "O Word of God Incarnate"

The Flame of His Joy

A bruised reed he will not break, and a
smoldering wick he will not snuff out.
In faithfulness he will bring forth justice.

Isaiah 42:3 NIV

*L*ife is not easy; in fact, some days,
even arising to face the day is a
truly daunting task. Because sin entered
the world and corrupted God's perfect
design, we may find ourselves bruised
like fragile reeds by the painful effects
of a broken world. If we allow ourselves
to stay in our broken state without
relying on the powerful source of God's
comfort, peace, and love, we might even
find ourselves as hopeless as a smoldering
wick about to lose its flame.

The state of hopelessness is dangerous; it is one of the worst places to allow ourselves to dwell. However, God knows our heartache, and he understands our suffering. When we have been bruised in this world, he offers us healing. We may never understand why we have to encounter heartbreaking experiences, but we can hold securely to the truth that God's justice is certain. He will heat our hearts with the flame of his joy again.

Power of Prayer

God, it's a quiet day. Help me pause to listen to you, to talk to you, to enjoy your company. Chase away my guilt and shame and fear, and draw me close to your heart. Remind me that no matter what my earthly roles may be, in your presence I am your child, and you care for me more than I could ever imagine. Let me lean against your heart now and hear it beating with love for me. Amen.

Prayer is needed for children and in families. Love begins at home and that is why it is important to pray together. If you pray together you will stay together and love each other as God loves each one of you.

—Mother Teresa of Calcutta

Stormy Times

*Not only so, but we also glory in our
suffering, because we know that suffering
produces perseverance; perseverance,
character; and character, hope.*

Romans 5:3–4 NIV

I am grateful, O God, for glimpses I
am given of you during times like
these. Thank you for showing me how,
during raging winds, the mother cardinal
refuses to move, standing like a mighty
shelter over the fledglings. Secure me
in the truth that I am likewise watched
over and protected during life's storms.

*Turmoil is the opposite of peace. We can
achieve inner peace by acknowledging our
turmoil, then shifting our focus toward
God's healing touch.*

Profound Humility

Humble yourselves before the Lord,
and he will exalt you.

James 4:10

The world we live in celebrates stardom, and the seemingly logical course of action is to promote ourselves like crazy to make sure we get our slice of the fame-and-fortune pie.

James's advice, however, sounds more like a serving of humble pie; who wants to eat that? That'll get you exactly nowhere...or so we may think. But, case in point, Jesus humbled himself in the most profound way, and the outcome of his humility is reigning forever as King of Kings and Lord of Lords.

We don't need to be afraid of walking in quietness and obscurity as we serve God with sincere hearts. He remembers every faithful step of our journey, and one day—whether on this side of eternity or the other—he will commend us.

We shall not grow wiser before we learn that much that we have done was very foolish.

—F. A. Hayek

Footing Regained

*The Lord is your keeper; the Lord is your
shade at your right hand. The sun shall not
strike you by day, nor the moon by night.*
Psalm 121:5–6

*L*ord, fear has reared its ugly head
again and is trying to take me
far away from you. Hold me close, Lord.
Even though I have momentarily lost my
footing in this world, please do not let
fear steal the peace I find in you. Give
me the strength to turn away from fear
and stand tall in the knowledge that I am
never alone.

*Fear knocked at the door. Faith answered.
No one was there.*
—Anonymous

Prayers from the Top

I have pleaded in prayer for you, Simon,
that your faith should not fail.

Luke 22:32 NIV

What a beautiful thing Jesus did for Simon Peter! He loved Peter so much that he prayed fervently that Peter's faith would remain strong. Is it possible Jesus pleads in prayer for us during our trials? If we desire it and believe that it is possible, why not? He may be pleading for us this very moment. Take courage in his supreme strength.

Hope knows that in the midst
of feeling all alone,
God is still with me.

One True Voice

I am the good shepherd.
I know my own and my own know me.

John 10:14

Your Word says—and I've heard it elsewhere too—that a flock of sheep knows its own shepherd's voice and won't respond to the voice of a different shepherd. It's true of my relationship with you too, Lord: I *know* your voice. I know when you're speaking to my heart, and I know when I'm being coaxed by "other voices"—wrong desires, worldly values, anxiety, pride, and the like. Thanks for helping me know the difference. Encourage me to follow the sound of your voice today and always.

Shine Your Light

Call to me and I will answer you,
and will tell you great
and hidden things that you
have not known.

Jeremiah 33:3

*L*ord, so often I keep doing the same things over and over and getting the same unsatisfying results. This is when I need you to shine your light on my life and reveal to me all that I haven't been able to see through my mortal eyes. You have all knowledge and every answer to the mysteries of heaven and earth. Please show me, Lord. Give me just a bit more of the knowledge you possess. Thank you.

Righteous in Christ

*The prayer of the righteous
is powerful and effective.*

James 5:16

oes this mean I need to seek
out a super saint when I need
real prayer power? Rarely do I consider
myself particularly righteous, but then I
remember that your Word says that I've
been *made* righteous in Christ. It's not
my righteousness that I'm counting on,
but his. That is reassuring and exciting!
So even *my* prayers, as I walk in Christ's
righteousness, can be powerful and
effective…right here and now!

A Gentle Approach

*And this is eternal life, that they may know
you, the only true God, and Jesus Christ
whom you have sent.*

John 17:3

*L*ord, I know I encounter them
every day: your loved ones who
are—on their own strength—desperately
trying to make some sense out of this
life. Help me reach out to them. Give me
the words to say and the gentle approach
that will lead them to the knowledge of
you and to the immense blessings you
want to bestow on them.

*Wherever I go and whoever I be,
let something of Jesus be seen in me.*

A Loving Refuge

How precious is your steadfast love, O God!
All people may take refuge in the shadow
of your wings.

Psalm 36:7

*L*ord, how grateful I am for the refuge your love provides. Your love never fails and never disappoints. Within the shelter of your love I am safe. Help me to love the people I encounter today as graciously as you love me, Lord. May they find in me the kind of forgiving, generous love that can only come from your presence in my life. Amen.

Weed Power

*The God who has girded me with strength
has opened wide my path.*

2 Samuel 22:33

*E*ven in my toughest moments,
Lord, I yearn to grow into fullest
flower. Help me find a faith as resilient
and determined as dandelions pushing up
through cracks in the pavement.

*Enliven my imagination, God of new life,
so that I can see through today's troubles
to coming newness. Surround me with
your caring so that I can live as if the new
has already begun.*

Held Fast
by Faithfulness

Righteousness will be his belt and
faithfulness the sash around his waist.

Isaiah 11:5 NIV

A sash or belt might not seem like a big deal today. In our fashion-savvy culture, these items are mainly worn as accessories. Though they might look nice, the belt and the sash are not mandatory elements of our wardrobe.

This was not the case long ago, when the belt and sash were necessities that held a person's garments securely to the body. The belt and sash kept the clothing in place.

34

So when Isaiah prophesied about Jesus, saying that his faithfulness would be a sash around his waist, we can rest assured that we are bound by Jesus' faithfulness. His faithfulness is not a mere sidenote; it is a vital aspect of his character. Even when our faith is shaken and we are close to losing all hope, he will never loosen his sash of faithfulness.

Lord, may I always keep in mind that you hold me fast with a secure sash of faithfulness.

Proving Grounds

He knows the way that I take; when he has
tested me, I shall come out like gold.

Job 23:10

It's good for me to be able to see
my difficulties as "proving grounds"
for my growing trust in you, Lord. From
difficulty finding fulfilling work to bills
I'm struggling to pay to a disagreement
with a loved one, life brings many
opportunities to look to you for help.
Today I put all of the "proving ground"
stuff I'm facing right now into your
hands, and I trust you with the outcome.

Faith isn't magic; it's a choice to trust
God, even when we are confused or sad.

No Distractions

I am the Lord, and there is no other;
besides me there is no god.

Isaiah 45:5

*L*ord, as I go about my day today, show me any "gods" I have placed before you. Help me to look honestly at how I spend my time and my money. Does one of these areas of investment reveal a strong allegiance to something other than you? If so, Lord, help me eradicate those distractions from my life.

We put our souls in God's hands because
we know that if God inspects them
regularly, they will work as they should.

—Archbishop Fulton Sheen

Led by His Spirit

For all who are led by the Spirit of God are children of God.

Romans 8:14

One sentiment I hear often is "We're all God's children." It's usually uttered during trying times, to remind us to hold on and keep the faith. The verse above stresses that God's children are led by his Spirit. May we strive each day to be active children of God, praying and following the call of his Spirit rather than our own impulses and desires.

The measure of a man's real character is what he would do if he knew he would never be found out.

—T. B. Macaulay

Heavenly Values

He will guard the feet of his faithful ones,
but the wicked shall be cut off in darkness;
for not by might does one prevail.

1 Samuel 2:9

The values of this world rarely seem to jibe with your values, Lord. I am in need of constant reminders not to get caught up in notions that status and physical appearance are of utmost importance. While society endorses such things, I know you say that lasting inner peace is achieved by faithfulness to you.

Lord, help me when I'm tempted
to believe that I can prevail in life
by being seen as "strong" in ways
that ultimately don't matter to you.

39

The Power and the Glory

To him belong the glory and the power
forever and ever. Amen.

1 Peter 4:11

*L*ord, in our world there is a great clamoring for power and glory, and we often see the inglorious results of someone's unethical attempts to get to the top. Protect us from such fruitless ambition—for we know it is only when we humble ourselves that you will lift us up higher than we could ever imagine.

Humility is the Christian's greatest honor;
and the higher men climb,
the further they are from heaven.

—Jane Porter

Just What We Need

My flesh and my heart may fail,
but God is the strength of my heart
and my portion forever.

Psalm 73:26

Lord, just when I was feeling exhausted and unsure about how I would make it through the day, I heard a praise song on the radio. It reminded me of the unending supply of strength that is ours through faith in you! Thanks for getting me through today, Lord. I would be so lost without you.

God always knows
just what we need,
and just when we need it.

41

Connected to You

*Those who are wise understand these
things; those who are discerning know
them. For the ways of the Lord are right,
and the upright walk in them,
but transgressors stumble in them.*

Hosea 14:9

I am here right now, Father, because
I do want to walk in your ways.
I know the key is staying connected
to you because the ways of the world
are all around me. Give me a wise and
discerning heart in all things today so I
can stay on track.

Surrounded by Wisdom

Whoever walks with the wise becomes wise,
but the companion of fools suffers harm.
Proverbs 13:20

*L*ord, help me to set a good
example and to be mindful of
the company I keep. I am not here to
judge, but I do want to keep company
with those who are using their time on
this earth in constructive rather than
wasteful ways. Help me to heed the
advice of those with more life experience
and—when called—to lead with a strong,
gentle example.

Wherever you are,
it is your friends who make your world.
—William James

Walk Uncompromised

Do not be conformed to this world,
but be transformed by the renewing
of your minds, so that you may discern
what is the will of God—what is good and
acceptable and perfect.

Romans 12:2

When I have one foot in the worldly scene and one foot in your kingdom, Lord, I'm compromising. Your ways of humility, love, and forgiveness are so at odds with worldly material values that there is no way to play both fields at once.

I have a choice to make. Do I choose to indulge in a lifetime of hedonistic pleasures, or will I choose to serve you, walking in your peaceful ways now and looking forward to the promise of eternity? I know what I choose, Lord. That's why I'm spending time with you right now. Help me to walk uncompromised today.

You can't sit on two chairs at once.
—Dutch Proverb

Grow in Christ

Grow in the grace and knowledge of our Lord and Savior Jesus Christ.

2 Peter 3:18

*G*rowing in the *grace* of Christ is to embrace all that he offers me in the way of love, mercy, and salvation. As I grow in his grace, I'll get better at extending love and mercy to others.

To grow in the *knowledge* of Christ is to spend time with him in prayer. As I spend more time with him, it will get easier to follow the example he set for us.

Precious Moments

*And we urge you, brothers, warn those
who are idle, encourage the timid,
help the weak, be patient with everyone.*

1 Thessalonians 5:14 NIV

*L*ord, help us to help each other
find you. Help us to not be too
sensitive to constructive criticism.

For my part, I ask your forgiveness
for the times I have polluted my mind
and spirit by choosing a questionable
form of entertainment over a more
life-affirming one. Protect me from
destructive habits, Lord. I know there
are better ways to spend my precious
moments on this earth.

Ongoing Dialogue

Rejoice always, pray without ceasing,
give thanks in all circumstances;
for this is the will of God
in Christ Jesus for you.

1 Thessalonians 5:16–18

How can I rejoice when I'm having "one of those days," Father? How can I pray continually when I feel overwhelmed?

When I look to Jesus' example, I find the answers I seek. He didn't stay on his knees 24/7, but he did maintain an ongoing dialogue with you. He acknowledged that he would prefer to avoid his cross, but he willingly took it up because it was necessary. He focused on the joy to come later, in due time.

I, too, can give thanks for the good things in my life, even when bad things are bearing down on me. I can keep up a dialogue with you as I go about my day, and I can be joyful in a deep, abiding sense, knowing that all is in your hands.

When we make joy, prayer,
and giving thanks our habit,
we are able to handle troubles
with courage and grace.

Faith on the Worst Days

For I know that my Redeemer lives,
And He shall stand at last on the earth;
And after my skin is destroyed, this I know,
That in my flesh I shall see God,
Whom I shall see for myself,
And my eyes shall behold, and not another.
How my heart yearns within me!

Job 19:25–27 NKJV

*L*ord, if my world were turned upside down in a single day like Job's was—losing everything I owned, and far worse—I doubt worship would be my instinctive response. But here is Job, recognizing himself as a mere man and praising you because you are God. He trusts your wisdom that reaches above and beyond his overwhelming tragedy. Somehow, he is able to understand that the blessings you gave him are not his to hold on to or that he can demand repayment from you. Even Job's punishing trials could not shake his faith in you.

Each prayer is a message of faith in God. We are saying, "I trust you; lead me. I believe in you; guide me. I need you; show me." When we offer ourselves openly, he will always answer.

Fresh Blessings

I do not hide your righteousness in my heart; I speak of your faithfulness and your saving help. I do not conceal your love and your faithfulness from the great assembly.
Psalm 40:10 NIV

When I think about your faithfulness to me, Lord, my heart overflows! I long to share this treasure trove with the people around me. When I consider all that you have done for me, I am overwhelmed by your love.

There are many aspects of life that are easy to take for granted: the air that I breathe, the rain for the crops, the food that I eat, and the relationships that I have. I sometimes forget how blessed I am. I want to take time every day to really contemplate how faithfully you work in my life. Once all of your blessings are fresh in my mind, it will be impossible to hide my gratitude. Your faithfulness will be on the tip of my tongue and in the innermost recesses of my heart.

Lord, I want to meditate on your blessings and share your faithfulness with the world.

Heart Maintenance

The Lord does not see as mortals see;
they look on the outward appearance,
but the Lord looks on the heart.

1 Samuel 16:7

This would be a great verse to hang over my bathroom mirror, Lord! As I work on my outward appearance each morning, help me to remember that my inner person needs attention too—and that's what you focus on. Your evaluation of my heart is more important to me than any human opinion of my appearance.

While you are proclaiming peace
with your lips, be careful to have it
even more fully in your heart.

—Francis of Assisi

Lead Me, Lord

*Commit your way to the Lord;
trust in him, and he will act.*

Psalm 37:5

*L*ord, this is one of those days when
I really don't know which way
to turn. I've lost my sense of direction
and feel as if I'm sitting on a rock in the
forest, wondering which trail will take
me back to familiar ground. Please lead
me, Lord. Send the signs I need to follow
to get to where you want me to go. I put
my trust in you.

*Let us pray not for lighter burdens
but for stronger backs.*
—Amish Proverb

Connected to the Lord

For my thoughts are not your thoughts,
nor are your ways my ways, says the Lord.
For as the heavens are higher than the
earth, so are my ways higher than your
ways and my thoughts than your thoughts.
Isaiah 55:8–9

Father, I am so grateful that your thoughts and your ways are so much higher than my own! Things in my life can be going along smoothly—and I may think I have everything under control—but it can all change in the blink of an eye. Help me stay connected with you, Lord, so that whether I'm enjoying smooth sailing or enduring high seas, I'll know I'm held fast by you.

Stop and Listen

Be still, and know that I am God!
I am exalted among the nations,
I am exalted in the earth.

Psalm 46:10

*L*ord, it often happens that you are trying to communicate an important truth to us, but we are so busy searching for the truth elsewhere that we don't stop and listen. Teach us the importance of being still, Lord. Only when we are still can we be aware of your presence and hear your voice. Only when we quiet the stirrings of our own souls can we connect with your will! Speak to us, Lord—and help us be ready to listen.

My Corner of
the Universe

*Those who oppress
the poor insult their Maker,
but those who are kind to
the needy honor him.*

Proverbs 14:31

I long to help every needy person in the world, Lord. Perhaps the most effective way to do this is by praying that you will send help wherever it is needed. Meanwhile, there is my corner of the universe with its many needs, some of which are surely within my reach: half my sandwich to the person standing near the freeway ramp with a sign; an evening spent going through my closet and setting aside items to donate; a weekend afternoon of helping with events at my church; a monthly visit to the sick, homebound, or imprisoned. It's a privilege to honor you by extending your compassion—in person.

Keep the light on
in your heart
so that those alone
in the dark
can find their way
home to God.

Trust in God

Do not worry, saying, "What will we eat?"
or "What will we drink?" or "What will
we wear?"...indeed your heavenly Father
knows that you need all these things.
But strive first for the kingdom of God and
his righteousness, and all these things will
be given to you as well.

Matthew 6:31–33

*P*rioritizing spiritual realities over temporal ones is not always easy. The physical realities are tangible. I can hold a stack of bills in my hand and know that if I don't pay them, problems will arise. But those spiritual realities... well, the benefits (and consequences) are not always so easy to recognize or see in the moment.

This is a faith issue, pure and simple. First, I need to stay calm about issues of provision. Second, I need to keep drawing near to you, Lord. Third, I need to reach out to others with your love. And after all of these things are done, I need to trust you with the results.

Since God has given me a cheerful heart,
I serve him with a cheerful spirit.
—Franz Joseph Haydn

Just Ask!

So I say to you, Ask, and it will be given
you; search, and you will find; knock, and
the door will be opened for you.
For everyone who asks receives,
and everyone who searches finds,
and for everyone who knocks,
the door will be opened.

Luke 11:9–10

*L*ord, I know you will show your
goodness and faithfulness to
me if I just diligently seek you. The
problem isn't your willingness to give
but my tendency to try to do everything
by myself rather than leaning on and
trusting in you. This silly inclination
brings me needless stress and wastes

precious time. Today I endeavor to lay
my needs and troubles at your feet
the minute I begin to feel the least bit
overwhelmed.

The words ask, search, *and* knock *start
with the letters* A, S, *and* K, *which spell*
ask. *We can use this little acrostic to
remind us to just* ask!

A Repaired Attitude

The wise woman builds her house, but the foolish tears it down with her own hands.

Proverbs 14:1

ord, why is it that frustration sometimes turns to despair and self-destruction? There are so many negative forces in the world as it is; why do I sometimes make a bad situation even worse because of my own bitter or hopeless attitude?

How often I wish I could take back thoughtless, hurtful words I have said to a loved one during the course of a particularly trying day! How many times I wish I could have a "do-over"! But there

are no "do-overs" in real life. Help me
make amends and handle things better
the next time I am challenged.

I have learned from experience that
the greater part of our happiness or misery
depends on our dispositions
and not on our circumstances.
—Martha Washington

Rest Assured

I will both lie down and sleep in peace;
for you alone, O Lord,
make me lie down in safety.

Psalm 4:8

How restful it is to live in your love, Lord God! In the middle of chaos or turmoil, I remember that you are with me, and I am at peace once again. When it seems as if everything is falling apart, you hold me close in your love, and I am able to sleep at night. There is no other source of peace like belonging to you, Father.

Faith, Hope, and Love

And now faith, hope, and love abide, these three; and the greatest of these is love.

1 Corinthians 13:13

My heavenly Father, what do I have to fear when you are the one caring for me? And yet, I do fear; irrationally I fear, despite your faithfulness, despite your assurances, and despite your promises. Why do I still fear? I don't always understand my trembling heart and the shadows of things far smaller than you before which it cowers. Please liberate me from these lapses of trust. Free me to stand fearlessly, supported by faith and hope, in the center of your great love for me.

Faith Versus Fear

*For this reason I remind you to rekindle
the gift of God that is within you ... for
God did not give us a spirit of cowardice,
but rather a spirit of power and of love
and of self-discipline.*

2 Timothy 1:6–7

Faith and fear cannot coexist. One
always gives way to the other. It is
necessary for us to be constantly building
up our faith to overcome the numerous
sources of destructive disbelief all around
us. We need to be continually working
at rekindling the gift of God that is in
us, which is our faith in him and in
his promises. We must be dedicated to

developing a spirit of love and power and discipline within ourselves.

Studying the words of the Scriptures, meditating on them, keeping God's commandments, and praying daily are some of the ways we can keep our faith strong. By focusing on these things, we shut out fear and cultivate faith.

Prayer is an aspiration of the heart, it is a simple glance directed toward heaven, it is a cry of gratitude and love in the midst of trial as well as joy.
—Thérèse of Lisieux

Peace Through Forgiveness

Teach me to do your will,
for you are my God. Let your good spirit
lead me on a level path.

Psalm 143:10

Lord, I know you want us to forgive those who do us wrong. In fact, you expect us to forgive because you set a sublime example by forgiving us first. Help me to forgive. Take away the hurt and betrayal, and leave only your peace.

The heart benevolent and kind
The most resembles God.

—Robert Burns

A Delicate Balance

Oh, the joys of those who trust the Lord,
who have no confidence in the proud
or in those who worship idols.

Psalm 40:4 NLT

Lord, if only all the false gods that lure us were clearly labeled. We are introduced to wealth, physical perfection, and romance—and it isn't until we realize that the pursuit of them is using up way too much of our resources that we discover we have made these things our gods. Help us to keep even good things in balance and never to pursue anything with more fervor than we pursue our relationship with you.

Nudges Toward Faith

Christ Jesus came into the world to save sinners—of whom I am the foremost.

1 Timothy 1:15

*L*ord, today a little white lie slipped so easily out of my mouth to save me from a trying commitment. As soon as I felt your little tug on my conscience, I knew I had to come clean about it and repair my relationship with you and with my friend.

I know that the lie wasn't small in your eyes, and it was a reminder to me that I am always vulnerable to sin. If I didn't feel your nudge to repair the situation as quickly as possible, I might have fallen into a complacency that would make me vulnerable to any number of more serious sins. I thank you for nudging me, Lord, and for forgiving me, yet again.

Even minor sin harms our relationships with God and others.

A Heart That Loves the Lord

Charm is deceitful, and beauty is vain,
but a woman who fears
the Lord is to be praised.

Proverbs 31:30

Lord, today I will be in the spotlight. I've been given an opportunity to be in front of a group, and I want to do a good job conveying my important message. Be with me, Lord; I know that I can accomplish very little without your help, but anything is possible with your guidance. Keep me focused not on myself, but on the insight I have to share.

Steady My Faith

Those of steadfast mind you
keep in peace—in peace because
they trust in you.

Isaiah 26:3

There is a unique toy on the market that reminds me of a mini Humpty Dumpty without legs. It is called a Weeble. The promotional jingle for it is "Weebles wobble, but they don't fall down!" Sometimes I feel like a Weeble, Lord, wobbling around—not falling, just unsteady in my faith. I know that my spiritual growth is a process, but I often get impatient. Please help me become more steadfast in trusting you. A bit less wobble will bring a lot more peace.

Faithful Listener

But it is for you, O Lord, that I wait; it is you, O Lord my God, who will answer.

Psalm 38:15

Sometimes my heart is so overwhelmed, God, that I don't know where to begin my prayer. Help me to quiet my soul and remember that you know everything inside of my mind before I ever come to you with it. Still, I need to tell you about it, Lord, and I know you want me to tell you. Thank you for being such a faithful listener and for caring about everything that concerns me. When I remember that, it helps me slow down, take a deep breath, and begin the conversation.

Darkest Before Dawn

Answer me when I call to you, O my righteous God. Give me relief from my distress; be merciful to me and hear my prayer.

Psalm 4:1 NIV

Teach me to know, God, that it is at my deepest despair that you are closest. At those times I can admit I have wandered in the dark, without a clue. Yet you have been there with me all along. Thank you for your abiding presence.

A despairing heart mumbles, "God is doing nothing." A hopeful heart inquires, "God, what are you going to do next?" and looks forward to celebrating God's awesome ingenuity.

Infuse My Spirit

*Let us run with perseverance the race
that is set before us, looking to Jesus the
pioneer and perfecter of our faith,
who for the sake of the joy that was set
before him endured the cross, disregarding
its shame, and has taken his seat
at the right hand of the throne of God.*

Hebrews 12:1–2

Some days the race feels like a sprint, Lord, and on other days, a marathon. On the harder days, please infuse my spirit with your strength and steadfastness. I want to run and finish well. Thank you for promising not to stop working until my faith is complete.

Peace for Troubled Minds

For thus said the Lord God,
the Holy One of Israel: In returning
and rest you shall be saved;
in quietness and in trust
shall be your strength.

Isaiah 30:15

ou, O Lord, are our refuge. When the days are too full and sleep is hard to come by, we simply need to escape to a quiet place and call on you. In your presence we find strength for our work and peace for our troubled minds. We are grateful for the comfort of your embrace, Lord.

One Day at a Time

*So do not worry about tomorrow, for
tomorrow will bring worries of its own.
Today's trouble is enough for today.*

Matthew 6:34

Keep me present in this day, Lord.
I know that yesterday is gone
and tomorrow isn't here yet, but my mind
rehashes what I did yesterday or wanders
to what I hope to do tomorrow. When I
worry about things I can't change, in the
past or the future, I lose the peace you
want me to have today. So thank you,
Lord, for going behind me and before me,
and for reminding me that living today to
the best of my ability is all you ask of me.
In your precious name I pray, amen.

No longer forward nor behind
I look in hope and fear;
But grateful take the good I find,
The best of now and here.
—John Greenleaf Whittier

Golden Opportunities

Martha was distracted by her many tasks;
so she...asked, "Lord, do you not care that
my sister has left me to do all the work by
myself? Tell her then to help me." But the
Lord answered her, "Martha, Martha, you
are worried and distracted by many things;
there is need of only one thing.
Mary has chosen the better part,
which will not be taken away from her."

Luke 10:40–42

I have Martha days and I have Mary days, Lord. Some days lend themselves more to a worshipful response to you than others do. But Mary didn't let everyday tasks distract her from a golden opportunity to glean wisdom from you, Lord. Help me in my quest to carve out time every day to be attentive to your Spirit. My to-do list will always be there on the back burner.

Thank you for including the Martha and Mary story in your Word, Lord. Many of us are like Martha, and I am grateful that you speak lovingly to us about our tendencies as you teach us to surrender to your peaceful ways.

The Privilege of Prayer

I urge that supplications,
prayers, intercessions, and thanksgivings
should be made for everyone, for kings and
all who are in high positions, so that
we may lead a quiet and peaceable life
in all godliness and dignity.

1 Timothy 2:1–2

Whether we keep an actual prayer list, a list in our heads, or no list at all, it is good to keep others in our prayers. We have the privilege of being able to pray for our family members, and what a relief it is to be able to entrust them to God's care when we feel disheartened or overwhelmed.

The passage at the top of the previous page reminds us to pray also for "all who are in high positions," which could include anyone from world leaders to our very own boss. Jesus even told us to pray for our enemies!

There isn't a soul on the face of the earth who doesn't need prayer, who doesn't need God's help in their lives. And who knows? Perhaps someone is praying for you too—right at this very moment.

Lord, please put on my heart and mind today the people who are most in need of prayer.

Jump In!

Into your hands I commit my spirit;
deliver me, Lord, my faithful God.

Psalm 31:5 NIV

I know that releasing control to you, Lord, is one of the hardest but most rewarding steps of obedience that I will ever take. Trusting in your faithfulness and submitting to your authority may seem like leaping headfirst into a river; I feel safe standing on the shoreline, looking at the roaring waves below, but I know I'm missing out on your best plans for my life. Yes, jumping into the river will sweep me away to places unknown—and it will take all of my strength and effort to navigate the waters—but the adventure will be so worth it!

I want to trust in your faithfulness. I believe that you have great things in store for me. You won't lead me down a river only to abandon me or leave me injured on the riverbed. My soul is precious to you, and you have a purpose in mind for my life. You are faithful, and I will claim that truth as I jump headfirst toward my destiny.

Take the first step in faith.
You don't have to see
the whole staircase.
Just take the first step.
—Dr. Martin Luther King Jr.

The Lord's Timetable

*With the Lord one day is like
a thousand years, and a thousand
years are like one day.*

2 Peter 3:8

Keep us from being slaves to time, Lord. Teach us to rest in the knowledge that time is in your hands. Whenever we think we don't have enough of it, show us you have plenty and are happy to share! Thank you, Lord, for your generous supply of time.

*You will never "find" time for anything.
If you want time you must make it.*
—Charles Buxton

A Faith Adventure

*Now faith is the assurance of things hoped
for, the conviction of things not seen.*

Hebrews 11:1

Human faith lives between two
extremes: It's neither completely
blind nor able to see everything. It has
plenty of evidence when it steps out and
trusts in God, but it takes each step with
a good many questions still unanswered.
It's really quite an adventure, this life
of faith. And Lord, I must confess that
experiencing your faithfulness over time
makes it easier and easier to trust you
with the unknown in life. Thank you for
your unshakable devotion.

Feet That Bring Good News

So they left the tomb quickly with fear and great joy, and ran to tell his disciples.

Matthew 28:8

*L*ord, how beautiful indeed are the feet that bring good news! I can't read the account of the women who visited your empty tomb without my heart beating a bit faster. As terrifying as the events preceding that first Easter morning were, how quickly utter grief turned into complete joy! Fill me with that joy, Lord. May it emanate from me and spread to others.

Awesome Creator

You are worthy, our Lord and God,
to receive glory and honor and power,
for you created all things, and by your will
they existed and were created.

Revelation 4:11

have trouble getting a single blade of grass to grow, Lord. By contrast, you created this entire universe and all it contains. If that doesn't inspire worship in my soul, I can't imagine what will. The truth is that it does put me in awe of you; it does stir my heart to join in the worship of heaven.

God created all things, and we are humbled and amazed at his magnificence.

Keep the Light Bright

You are the light of the world...
let your light shine before others,
so that they may see your good works
and give glory to your Father in heaven.

Matthew 5:14, 16

*J*esus, you said these words to your
followers, and they echo down
through the centuries to meet me here,
as I turn my heart toward you in prayer.

I think of the times and ways your light
has shined brightly through me. I'm also
aware of things I do and say—as well as
the attitudes I sometimes have—that dim
or obscure that light at times.

Please trim the wick of my words today,
clean the glass chimney of my attitudes,
and add the fuel of good behavior to this
lamp that is my life in you.

*It takes only one lamp in a dark place
to demonstrate the beauty
and benefit of light.*

Eyes on the Prize

For this slight momentary affliction is preparing us for an eternal weight of glory beyond all measure, because we look not at what can be seen but at what cannot be seen; for what can be seen is temporary, but what cannot be seen is eternal.

2 Corinthians 4:17–18

How can any affliction be considered slight? But then, it was the Apostle Paul who wrote these words. Paul was whipped, beaten, and almost killed by rock-throwing antagonists. Several times the victim of shipwrecks, Paul was exposed to the elements, then imprisoned and abandoned by friends who couldn't take the heat.

But because Paul believed his future in Christ would hold great wonder and blessings, his passing hardships were of little consequence to him. He had his eyes on the prize, and in light of his goal, everything he had to go through to reach it was worth it.

Alexander, Caesar, Charlemagne and I have founded empires. But upon what did we rest the creation of our genius? Upon force. Jesus Christ founded his empire upon love; and at this hour millions of men would die for him.

—Napoleon Bonaparte

Letting God Lead

*You who have made me see many troubles
and calamities will revive me again; from
the depths of the earth you will bring me
up again. You will increase my honor, and
comfort me once again.*

Psalm 71:20–21

Lord, a vexing situation has me
very confused. Is it possible I'm
trying to sort it out through my own
limited understanding and overlooking a
crucial element? I know I can trust you
with anything. I give this up to you and
ask you to restore me to a place where I
can look at what's going on in the right
way—your way.

How often we look upon God as our last and feeblest resource! We go to him because we have nowhere else to go. And then we learn that the storms of life have driven us, not upon the rocks, but into the desired haven.

—George MacDonald

Present in All Places

Where can I go from your spirit?
Or where can I flee from your presence?
If I ascend to heaven, you are there;
if I make my bed in Sheol, you are there.
If I take the wings of the morning
and settle at the farthest limits
of the sea, even there your hand shall
lead me, and your right hand
shall hold me fast.

Psalm 139:7–10

The threat "You can run but you can't hide" gets turned on its head in this passage—transformed into a promise of God's presence with us in all places. The Lord isn't ever going to be left behind when we're in a place that seems distant or unfamiliar. In fact, he's already there. It's a great truth to keep in mind, whether we're headed to the dentist today or on a trip around the world.

For those who trust in God,
the safest place in the world
is wherever he leads us.

Small Is Good

O Lord, be gracious to us; we wait for you.
Be our arm every morning, our salvation in
the time of trouble.

Isaiah 33:2

Into the bleakest winter of my soul, Lord, you are tiptoeing. May I drop whatever I'm doing and accept this gesture so it may not get overlooked in my frantic search for something massive and overwhelming. Remind me that it is not you who demands lavish celebrations and strobe-lit displays of faith. Rather, you ask only that I have the faith of a mustard seed. I am ready.

Even now I am full of hope,
but the end lies in God.

—Pindar

Ups and Downs

When times are good, be happy; but when times are bad, consider: God has made the one as well as the other.

Ecclesiastes 7:14 NIV

Help me understand, O God, that we can't have good without bad—a head without a tail. Help me remember the joy when grief strikes my heart. For just as it takes a negative to create a photograph, it takes dark and light to complete creation. Therein lies the promise: Darkness is only half of the portrait of life.

When the darkness casts shadows upon us and the answers are nowhere in sight, hope lifts us up on a wing and a prayer and carries us back to the light.

Clear Out the Clutter

If you abide in me, and my words
abide in you, ask for whatever you wish,
and it will be done for you.

John 15:7

*L*ord, I want so much to abide in
you. I desire to have you abiding
in me as well—and so closely that I can
feel your presence and speak to you
at any time. Help me to ignore the
distractions that create distance between
us. Clear out the clutter that keeps me
from sensing your best plan for my life.

We know the truth,
not only by the reason,
but also by the heart.

—Blaise Pascal

The Essence of Worship

God is spirit, and those who worship him must worship in spirit and truth.

John 4:24

A phrase that has popped up in the Christian music market recently is "extreme worship." Many things in our culture are moving toward extreme versions of themselves. We have extreme sports, extreme home improvement shows, and *now* extreme worship.

What God is looking for, though, is not found in our form—it's found in the essence of our worship. It's not something anyone can identify by the *appearance* of a worshipper—it's something only God can see when he examines our hearts.

Speech Without Words

The heavens are telling
the glory of God; and the firmament
proclaims his handiwork. Day to day
pours forth speech, and night to night
declares knowledge. There is no speech,
nor are there words; their voice
is not heard; yet their voice goes out
through all the earth, and their words
to the end of the world.

Psalm 19:1–4

Creation shouts to me, Lord, about
how amazing you
are. I see the wonder
of your wisdom in
everything from
the solar system

to how bodies of water feed into one another to the life cycles of all living creatures. Everywhere I turn there is something that makes me think about how creative and insightful you are.

Thank you for this universe that speaks without words. I hear it loud and clear, and it tells me of your magnificence.

*There's nothing like
an hour or two of stargazing
to regain perspective
on the greatness
and goodness of God.*

High-Quality Works

And whatever you do, in word or deed,
do everything in the name of
the Lord Jesus, giving thanks to God
the Father through him.

Colossians 3:17

*L*ooking at almost any product in the store, shoppers can find some kind of indication of where the item was manufactured: "Made in Taiwan" or "Product of Canada" or "Handcrafted in India" are just a few of the designations out there in consumer land.

Some manufacturers are known for high-quality materials and craftsmanship, while others are known for taking any shortcut to offer lower prices.

Similarly, whatever Christians say and do goes out into the world stamped with Jesus' name on it. What kind of a reputation will our contributions to his name build in our corner of the world today? We should make sure our works follow the example he set for us.

> *Let us endeavor so to live that when we come to die even the undertaker will be sorry.*
> —Mark Twain

Sure Belief

When the angels had left them and gone into heaven, the shepherds said to one another, "Let us go now to Bethlehem and see this thing that has taken place, which the Lord has made known to us."

Luke 2:15

Seeing is believing, right? But from what is recorded of the shepherds' dialogue, it appears that they already believed what the angel told them; they were making a beeline to Bethlehem *because* of their belief, not to establish it. What a wonderful faith they had!

Father, I want my faith to be like the shepherds': trusting you and taking positive action based on your Word.

108

The One and Only God

Yours, O Lord, are the greatness,
the power, the glory, the victory,
and the majesty; for all that is in the
heavens and on the earth is yours.

1 Chronicles 29:11

*L*ord, do we tell you often enough how awesome you are? We stand in complete awe of your power. Let us never underestimate your ability to change our reality in an instant, even when it involves moving mountains or calming storms. You are the one and only God, and we give you glory at all times.

If God is willing to move
your mountain, don't tell
him where to put it.

God's Purposes

Now to him who by the power at work
within us is able to accomplish abundantly
far more than all we can ask or imagine,
to him be glory in the church and in Christ
Jesus to all generations, forever and ever.
Amen.

Ephesians 3:20–22

Father, sometimes I see people who seem to have found work perfectly suited to them, and I wonder if I am fulfilling my purpose. Thank you for reminding me that you are at work in me, bringing about your purposes, which are not always clear to me. You take even small gifts—as you did with the loaves and the fishes—and you make them multiply.

Help Me See the Good

For everything created by God is good,
and nothing is to be rejected, provided
it is received with thanksgiving; for it is
sanctified by God's word and by prayer.
1 Timothy 4:4–5

Does this apply to the most annoying gnats, Lord? What about mean people and cold-blooded killers? Sometimes it is hard to see the good. Help me to do my part with love, then pray over and give up the more confounding elements to you.

Saying a small prayer whenever we are
troubled helps us remember that though
there are many things beyond our grasp,
all is in God's hands.

Live by Faith

*For in it the righteousness of God
is revealed through faith for faith;
as it is written, "The one who is righteous
will live by faith."*

Romans 1:17

Faith is more than a passive idea; it is a principle of action that motivates our day-to-day decisions and actions. Would a farmer plant if he did not expect to harvest? Would the student read and study if she did not believe it would improve the quality of her life? Would we work hard each day if we did not hope that by doing so we might accomplish something worthwhile?

We daily act upon things we believe in, though we cannot yet see the end result. This is the faith we live by, whether we identify it as such or not.

As faithful people, we take this principle one step further: We do things that are motivated by our faith in things promised but not yet fulfilled. We smile in the face of adversity. We continue in prayer even when our prayers don't seem to be answered. We stop saying, "I can't" and start believing God can! Step by step, we put our faith into action and learn to "live by faith."

All That We Think We Know

*"Truly I tell you, whoever does not receive
the kingdom of God as a little child
will never enter it." And he took
[the children] up in his arms, laid his
hands on them, and blessed them.*

Mark 10:15–16

*L*ord, when I speak to others about
my faith, sometimes I see doubt
in their faces. Faith doesn't always seem
to make sense to the "rational" adult in
us, unfortunately.

Please give us the grace that will enable
us to come to you with open minds, open
hearts—and open arms. I know that once

we clear our minds of all that we think
we know, all will become clear to us
through you.

> *Being childlike isn't the same*
> *as being childish. Childishness*
> *would point to a lack of maturity,*
> *a lack of self-control, and a tendency*
> *toward foolishness. Childlikeness has*
> *to do with being innocent, humble,*
> *and full of love and awe.*

Pray Without Ceasing

Devote yourselves to prayer,
keeping alert in it with thanksgiving.

Colossians 4:2

*L*ord, if all the prayers ever prayed
were linked together, surely
they would reach to heaven and back
countless times! We want to be a people
who pray without ceasing, Lord. Hear
both the prayers we utter and the silent
prayers of our hearts.

Prayer is not monologue, but dialogue;
God's voice in response to mine
is its most essential part.

—Andrew Murray

Meager Offerings

Ascribe to the Lord the glory due his name;
bring an offering, and come before him.

1 Chronicles 16:29

*L*ord, no matter what we bring of
ourselves to give you, even if we
include all our hopes and dreams, it's
never enough to give in return for all
you've given to us. And so we give you
our praise. We sing to you and come
before you with our meager offerings,
praying all the while that you will make
something marvelous of them.

God's gifts put man's
best dreams to shame.
—Elizabeth Barrett Browning

Endless Joy

Father, thank you for initiating our wonderful relationship by loving me first! Your perfect love has taught me to trust you and leave my fear of your judgment behind. Your love for me brings such joy to my life, Lord. Help me spread this joy to others today.

Love is not abstract—it's concrete. It's the reality of self-sacrifice rather than self-preservation, of giving even when it hurts, of forgiving rather than "keeping score."

Because of You

What then are we to say about these things? If God is for us, who is against us?

Romans 8:31

Lord of my heart, give me a refreshing drink from the fountains of your love, walking through this desert as I have. Lord of my heart, spread out before me a new vision of your goodness, locked into this dull routine as I am. Lord of my heart, lift up a shining awareness of your will and purpose, awash in doubts and fears though I be.

Hope is the parent of faith.

—Cyrus Augustus Bartol

A Self-Checkup

Let us test and examine our ways,
and return to the Lord. Let us
lift up our hearts as well as our hands
to God in heaven.

Lamentations 3:40–41

The idea of an exam can strike fear in even prepared individuals. But the exam to which God's Word calls us is different from any math final or set of philosophical questions. It is a self-checkup—a chance to ask ourselves probing questions and answer them honestly. If we give ourselves some not-so-good marks, we don't need to become discouraged. Instead, we can use what we learn to initiate a fresh starting point for getting back into fellowship with God.

A Model of Good Works

*Show yourself in all respects
a model of good works.*

Titus 2:7

*L*ord, thank you for calling me
to yourself and giving me your
Spirit to strengthen me—heart, soul,
mind, and body—to work in ways that
bring honor to you. This goal of being
a model of good works in every respect
makes me realize how much I need you
each moment. As I grow in a life of
doing what is right and
true and good, help me
grow in humility as well,
remembering that you
are the source of my
strength.

The Shield of Faith

*With all of these, take the shield of faith,
with which you will be able to quench all
the flaming arrows of the evil one.*

Ephesians 6:16

There is an opposition in all things,
and there are all kinds of life
circumstances that can erode our faith.

What are some "flaming arrows" that
might come in our direction? Doubt
and fear, sadness and depression?
Temptations, both to the body and
the spirit? What about financial
and employment problems, marriage
problems, and health problems?

All these and more might be the "flaming arrows" spoken of in the Bible. But we must remember we have faith as our shield! A shield is a versatile and effective means of defense in any battle we might face. Our faith, if it is built upon Christ and his teachings, can defend us against any onslaught.

Don your armor today—
and don't forget your shield of faith!

Unfairness

For the Lord loves justice; he will not forsake his faithful ones.

Psalm 37:28

*L*ife's not fair, and I'm so frustrated. The powerful get more so as the rest of us shrink, dreams for peace are shattered as others get the upper hand. Despair is too tempting. Help me hold on, for you are a God of justice and dreams, of turning life upside down. Show me the way; thanks for listening in the meantime.

A calm spirit pours water on the hottest fire.

God's Grace

O God, your love is so great. I'm not sure that I can love as you do or even love others in a way that will please you. God, teach me how to really love my family, my friends, and even strangers. I trust in the power of your love to make me into a far more loving person than I am today. Amen.

When God's love is seen in my relationships with friends and family, the world gets a glimpse of God's saving grace.

Humiliation Versus Humility

Pride ends in humiliation,
while humility brings honor.

Proverbs 29:23 NLT

*S*omeone may ask, "What's the difference between humility and humiliation?" A simple way to look at it is that humility is voluntary and peaceful, while humiliation is compulsory and painful.

Practically speaking, it's better for me to think rightly about myself in relation to God and others (i.e., to walk in humility) than to think I'm "all that" and experience the humiliation of an extreme reality check.

As I walk in true humility, there's the added bonus that God will send honor my way—and the honor he will set up for me will be sweeter than any I could try to grab for myself.

*Lord, please show me
my blind spots of pride
so I can choose
the path of humility now
and avoid the pain
of humiliation later.*

Precious Freedom

Now the Lord is the Spirit, and where the Spirit of the Lord is, there is freedom.

2 Corinthians 3:17

*L*ord, how blessed we are to be able to worship as we please. Help us to never take such freedom for granted. Today we ask you to bless any believers who are being persecuted for living out their faith. Draw especially near to them, Lord. Surround them with your mighty army of angels.

*Long may our land be bright
with freedom's holy light;
protect us by Thy might,
Great God, our King!*

—Samuel F. Smith

A Well-Kept Path

For who is God, but the Lord? And who is a rock, except our God? The God who has girded me with strength has opened wide my path. He made my feet like the feet of deer, and set me secure on the heights.

2 Samuel 22:32–34

Trying to tackle life without God is like making your way alone through a jungle filled with perils. It is rough going—discouraging, disheartening, and often disastrous. The life of faith, on the other hand, is one of being led on a well-kept path. Even though trouble may come along, it cannot overwhelm us because the Lord strengthens and guards our souls when we call on him for help.

My Rock

There is no Holy One like the Lord, no one besides you; there is no Rock like our God.

1 Samuel 2:2

*L*ord, please keep me from falling into the trap of placing any other human on a pedestal. Even the most spiritual-seeming religious leaders are riddled with imperfection; they struggle with sin, just as I do. You alone are perfect and pure, and you alone are worthy of my adoration. I promise I will not follow anyone else, no matter how spiritually enlightened they may seem. There is no one like you, and you are the only one who will ever have my full devotion.

The Barriers Inside

You are indeed my rock and my fortress;
for your name's sake lead me and guide me.
Psalm 31:3

Lord, I wish to live a long life, but I fear growing old. I want to accomplish great things, but I fear risking what I already have. I desire to love with all my heart, but the prospect of self-revelation makes me shrink back. Perhaps for just this day, would you help me reach out? Let me bypass these dreads and see instead your hand reaching back to mine—right now—just as it always has.

Faith has moved mountains, healed hearts, and saved men from the sword. With this power we need not search for answers outside of the Lord.

God's Faithfulness

Remember his covenant forever,
the word that he commanded,
for a thousand generations.

1 Chronicles 16:15

*A*lmighty God, our faith in you is undergirded by your faithfulness. No matter how many times we turn away, you patiently wait for us to return to you. Instill in us that same sense of honor and faithfulness that is yours, Lord. May we be as faithful to you as you have been to us.

God always was, is now,
and always will be faithful.

Strength of Character

The Lord God helps me; therefore
I have not been disgraced; therefore
I have set my face like flint, and
I know that I shall not be put to shame.

Isaiah 50:7

Sometimes doing the right thing takes more guts than I feel able to muster, Lord. If I do what I know I should, people might get angry or exclude me. Help me, Lord! Give me the strength of character to follow you, even when it makes me unpopular for a while. I entrust the end result to you.

My Provision and My Protection

Unless the Lord builds the house,
those who build it labor in vain.
Unless the Lord guards the city, the guard
keeps watch in vain. It is in vain that you
rise up early and go late to rest,
eating the bread of anxious toil;
for he gives sleep to his beloved.

Psalm 127:1–2

Sometimes I try to do too much by my own efforts, Father. Thank you for this reminder that everything I do to further my own cause and ensure my own safety isn't going to be effective apart from an abiding trust in you.

Help me remember, too, that you aren't just some magic charm to hedge all my bets. Forgive me for the times I've treated you like that! You are my provision and my protection—you are my very life.

Thank you, Lord, for the peace of mind that always comes when I stop trying to do everything myself and tap into your unending supply of strength.

God asks little, but He gives much.
—John Chrysostom

Patience to Endure

Let endurance have its full effect,
so that you may be mature and complete,
lacking in nothing.

James 1:4

*L*ord, we are a people in search of a shortcut. Give us the five-minute dinner preparation and the instant credit! But we know, because you are so clear about this in your Word, that a mature faith can't be achieved overnight. Give us patience to endure, Lord. We are determined to become the complete individuals you intended us to be.

It takes a great deal of time and pressure for a piece of coal to become a diamond.

Available for His Purposes

I am the Lord your God; sanctify yourselves therefore, and be holy, for I am holy.

Leviticus 11:44

When I was younger, I used to think that *sanctify* meant something akin to "sanitize." I thought God was calling me to clean up my act in this verse. But *sanctify* actually means "set apart," and in this case it means "set apart to God." It's a call for me to commit myself to God, to put myself in his hands, to be available for his purposes. Then, as I give myself to him, he makes me able to walk in holiness.

Stand Strong

Do not let loyalty and faithfulness
forsake you; bind them around your neck,
write them on the tablet of your heart.

Proverbs 3:3

Lord, how I long to stand strong
in faith! I read of great people
of faith and question my own courage.
Would I, if my life depended on it, say,
"Yes, I believe in God"? I pray I would.
Prepare me for any opportunity to
stand firm for what I know to be true.
To live without conviction is hardly to
live at all.

I am not afraid...I was born to do this.
—Joan of Arc

Faith to Do Your Will

*O Most High, when I am afraid, I put my
trust in you. In God, whose word I praise,
in God I trust; I am not afraid;
what can flesh do to me?*

Psalm 56:2–4

Lord, I know that it was not David's
sling that won the victory against
Goliath—it was David's trust in you.
While the other troops cowered in the
camp because of Goliath's threats and
taunts, David ran out to meet the giant
in your name. Oh, Lord, I want to be like
David. I don't want to cower in fear; I
want to run out in faith to do your will.

Making New Places for God

For your steadfast love is before my eyes,
and I walk in faithfulness to you.

Psalm 26:3

Change is inevitable, Lord, we know. Help us to accept those changes: If we view each transition as an opportunity to experience your faithfulness, we make new places in our lives for spiritual growth.

God's protective love is a praiseworthy blessing.

Standing Tall

Now to him who is able to keep you from falling…to the only God our Saviour, through Jesus Christ our Lord, be glory, majesty, power, and authority, before all time and now and for ever. Amen.

Jude 24–25

Lord, I want to tell you how much I love you, how grateful I am that you have taken me into your care. Ever since I've entrusted myself to you, you've kept me from becoming entangled in things that would bring me to ruin. You fill my heart with peace as I stay close to you. It's a miracle of your grace that I am standing tall today, lifting my praise to you from a heart full of love.

Relationship with God

*For I know that my Redeemer lives, and
that at the last he will stand upon the
earth; and after my skin has been thus
destroyed, then in my flesh I shall see God.*

Job 19:25–26

When Job spoke the above
words, his body was covered
with painful boils. After losing all
his possessions, Job was enduring the
deterioration of his health and grieving
over the loss of his children. Job had
always walked uprightly before God,
and all of these evils had befallen him
nonetheless. How disheartening!

Still, even while Job was immersed in
pain and on the brink of death, his faith

in God did not waver. By focusing on his Redeemer and the eternal life he knew was ahead for him, Job refused to allow anything to rob him of his relationship with God.

For Jesus Christ I am prepared to suffer still more.

—Maximilian Kolbe

Going It Alone

*Praise be to the God and Father of our Lord
Jesus Christ, the Father of compassion and
the God of all comfort, who comforts us
in all our troubles, so that we can comfort
those in any trouble with the comfort we
ourselves receive from God.*

2 Corinthians 1:3–4 NIV

Time helps, Lord, but it never quite
blunts the loneliness that loss brings.
Thank you for the peace that is slowly
seeping into my pores, allowing me to live
with the unlivable, to bear the unbearable.

Guide and bless my faltering steps down
a new road. Prop me up when I think I
can't go it alone; prod me when I tarry
too long in lonely self-pity.

Most of all, Kind Healer, thank you for the gifts of memory and dreams. The one comforts, the other beckons, both halves of a healing whole.

Days of Miracles

*He replied, "What is impossible
for mortals is possible for God."*

Luke 18:27

*O*nly faith can look past a seemingly
impossible situation and believe
that it will change. I believe you are a
God of miracles, Lord. These are days
of miracles, as were the days of Noah,
Moses, and Joseph. I may not see the seas
parted, peoples freed, or congregations
caught up to heaven, but through faith I
expect wonderful gifts from you. I believe
that with you, all things are possible!

Work for the Lord

*Let the favor of the Lord our God be upon
us, and prosper for us the work of our
hands—O prosper the work of our hands!*

Psalm 90:17

Lord, so often the difference
between a productive workday
and a fruitless one lies in our attitude.
When we truly work as if working for
you, it makes such a difference! Forgive
us, Lord, for those times when we dig
into our tasks without bringing you into
the situation as well. Whether it's peeling
potatoes, pulling weeds, or writing a
screenplay, we want to tune in to your
power to perfect our work on this earth.

A Way Out

No testing has overtaken you that is not common to everyone. God is faithful, and he will not let you be tested beyond your strength, but with the testing he will also provide the way out so that you may be able to endure it.

1 Corinthians 10:13

I am extremely grateful that every temptation has an escape hatch, Lord. I want to be a woman who is in the habit of looking for the way out of a tempting circumstance, not lingering in the snare zone.

No matter how powerful a lure might be, please help me resist the bait. Keep reminding me that your ways are best. They are filled with peace and satisfaction, and they never leave a trace of regret lingering in my soul.

How to escape temptation:
Step one: Look for an escape route. (Pray!)
Step two: Take the escape route. (Run!)
Step three: Enjoy your freedom. (Dance!)

Around the Bend

You are a hiding place for me; you preserve me from trouble; you surround me with glad cries of deliverance.

Psalm 32:7

I'm getting a crick in my neck trying to see around the bend, God of past and future. I'm wearing myself out second-guessing. Teach me to live in today—my eyes only on you—needing just a small glimpse down the road. No need to borrow trouble that may not be waiting.

Through faith we learn that the impossible is possible, that dreams can become reality, and that miracles do happen.

Tears and Laughter

Lord, often when a loved one dies, the tears and laughter get all mixed up together. The absence of the person makes us reflect on the good times we shared with them, and laughter interrupts our tears. I think that's your way of helping us begin to heal, Lord. Help us to revel in the laughter when it comes and let the tears flow when necessary. If we lean on each other and on you, we can move through grief in a life-affirming way.

Lord, we do not complain because you have taken him from us, but rather we will thank you for having given him to us.
—Angelo Sodano

A World Bursting with Hope

The living, the living—they praise you, as I am doing today; parents tell their children about your faithfulness.

Isaiah 38:19 NIV

Speaking of God's faithfulness can be difficult; it might even seem weird to talk about God at times. But we can make talking about God and all that he has done for us a habit that we weave into our daily lives. We can take a step of faith and start speaking about God to someone close to us, even if we feel a bit unsure at first.

An easy way to start is to choose one faithful work that God has done in our lives and confide in one person today. The more of God's faithfulness we begin to share, the more God's faithfulness will be apparent in our world, and the more we will notice it.

Once we get over our fear of sharing and finally find joy in speaking about God, we'll soon see that our little "God-talks" are helping us and others too. We will see all the blessings that surround us with fresh eyes and then we will see a world bursting with hope.

God can't give us happiness and peace apart from Himself, because it is not there. There is no such thing.
—C. S. Lewis

Faith in Love

O God, who art the truth, make me one with Thee in continual love! I am weary often to read and hear many things. In Thee is all that I desire and long for. Let all teachers hold their peace; let all creatures be silent in Thy sight; speak to me alone.

—Thomas à Kempis, *The Imitation of Christ*

When confusion sets in, and when there is too much advice coming from too many places, don't forget God, his wisdom, and his love.

Start the Day Right

In the morning, while it was still very dark,
he got up and went out to a deserted
place, and there he prayed.

Mark 1:35

*L*ord, how many times have I resolved to spend time first thing each morning in your Word and in prayer—and how many times have I neglected to do so! A day that begins with you is sure to be a day blessed by you. Give me an insatiable thirst for time with you, Lord. Thank you for always being available to meet with me.

Soak in Wisdom

*It is better to hear the rebuke of the wise
than to hear the song of fools.*

Ecclesiastes 7:5

I do sometimes prefer frivolity
to growing in the light of some
uncomfortable truth, Lord. You know
when I'm indulging in foolishness
when I could be having a meaningful
interaction with someone who walks
in the truth. I know it's okay to enjoy
this marvelous life you've given me, but
it's good for me to look in the mirror
regularly as well. Grant me the grace to
soak in the wisdom that will change me
for the better.

Immersed in Your Word

Turn my eyes from looking at vanities;
give me life in your ways.

Psalm 119:37

*L*ord, how many distractions there
are in this world! How easy it is
to get caught up in the desire to acquire.
How tempting to read one self-help book
after another, until I am dizzy. I know
that true contentment, true beauty, and
true wisdom are found only in your Word.
Keep me focused on the right things.

To reach something good
it is very useful to have gone astray,
and thus acquire experience.

—Teresa of Avila

Strength and Stability

*L*ord, you are the foundation of my life. When circumstances shift and make my world unsteady, you remain firm. When threats of what lies ahead blow against the framework of my thoughts, you are solid. When I focus on your steadfastness, I realize that you are my strength for the moment, the one sure thing in my life. Because of you I stand now, and I will stand tomorrow as well, because you are there already. Amen.

Stay focused on how to best serve the present by keeping your foundation strong, and the future ultimately will prosper.

—Vivian Elisabeth Glyck, *12 Lessons on Life I Learned from My Garden*

Help My Unbelief!

Jesus said to him, "If you are able!—
All things can be done for the one who
believes." Immediately the father of the
child cried out, "I believe;
help my unbelief!"

Mark 9:23–24

All of us face difficult hours in our lives—hours when in tears we fall to our knees and plead something similar to what this father uttered. Just as the Lord stood ready to help this father, so he is ready to assist us today.

Lord, thank you for your perfect love.
Please take the humble offering
of my feeble faith and make it strong
through your sustaining power.

Acknowledgments:

The University of Chicago Press: lines from *The Odes of Pindar*, translated by Richmond Lattimore, copyright 1947 by The University of Chicago.

Unless otherwise noted, all Scripture quotations are taken from the *New Revised Standard Version* of the Bible. Copyright © 1989 National Council of the Churches of Christ in the United States of America. Used by permission. All rights reserved.

Scripture quotations marked NIV are taken from *The Holy Bible, New International Version*®, NIV®. Copyright © 1973, 1978, 1984 by Biblica, Inc.™ Used by permission of Zondervan. All rights reserved worldwide. www.zondervan.com

Scripture quotations marked NLT are taken from the *Holy Bible, New Living Translation*, copyright © 1996, 2004, 2007 by Tyndale House Foundation. Used by permission of Tyndale House Publishers, Inc., Carol Stream, Illinois 60188. All rights reserved.